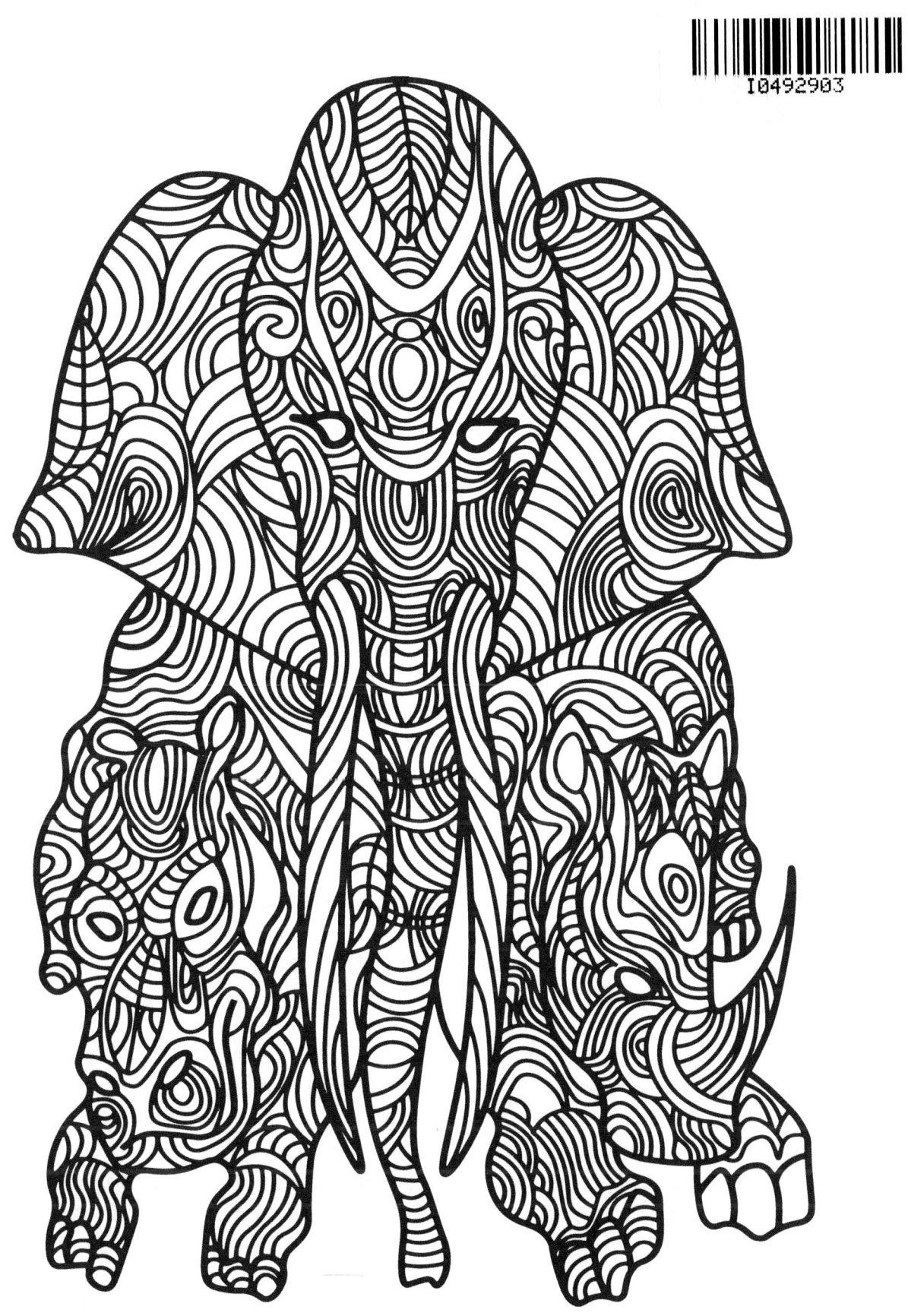

The king of the big cats, the lion, is a force to be reckoned with. It is without the shadow of a doubt, nature at its finest.

The outcry over the death of Cecil the lion, illegally hunted and killed by an American dentist, outraged the internet. But, what really is outrageous, is that these incredible creatures could be extinct within our lifetimes.

In the last 50 years, the African lion has dwindled by 75%, falling from around 100,000 to 32,000 today, and these numbers may be hugely optimistic. The drop is entirely due to humans: we are destroying their natural habitat, the savannah, even more quickly than the tropical rain forests.

Cecil was just one of hundreds of lions killed for sport. More than 600 lions are killed every year by trophy hunting tourists. That's 2% of the population every year, with adult males being disproportionately targeted.

With the right permits in th right areas, killing lions is perfectly legal. The lion populaion is currently threatened but not deemed endangered, if so then all hunting would be deemed illegal. This is what many conservationists want to see so that the species can be saved.

Of course, there will always be illegal hunting no matter what the law states, and this is what needs to be tackled sooner rather than later.

The life of a lion is hard enough, without facing poaching and decline of habitat, education is very important so that we can keep them safe and thus ensuring their survival.

Despite what the pro-hunting organizations might have you believe, only 3% of the revenues from hunting goes to local communities.

Lions have already been wiped out in some areas. In 2005, thousands of West African lions were believed to live in 21 different locations. In 2014, they only live in four areas, and there are just 400 West African lions left.

So, lions are really an endangered species and could become extinct in fewer than 20 years, the government need to do something about this now and declare them as such.

To lose the lion from this Earth would be a tragedy.

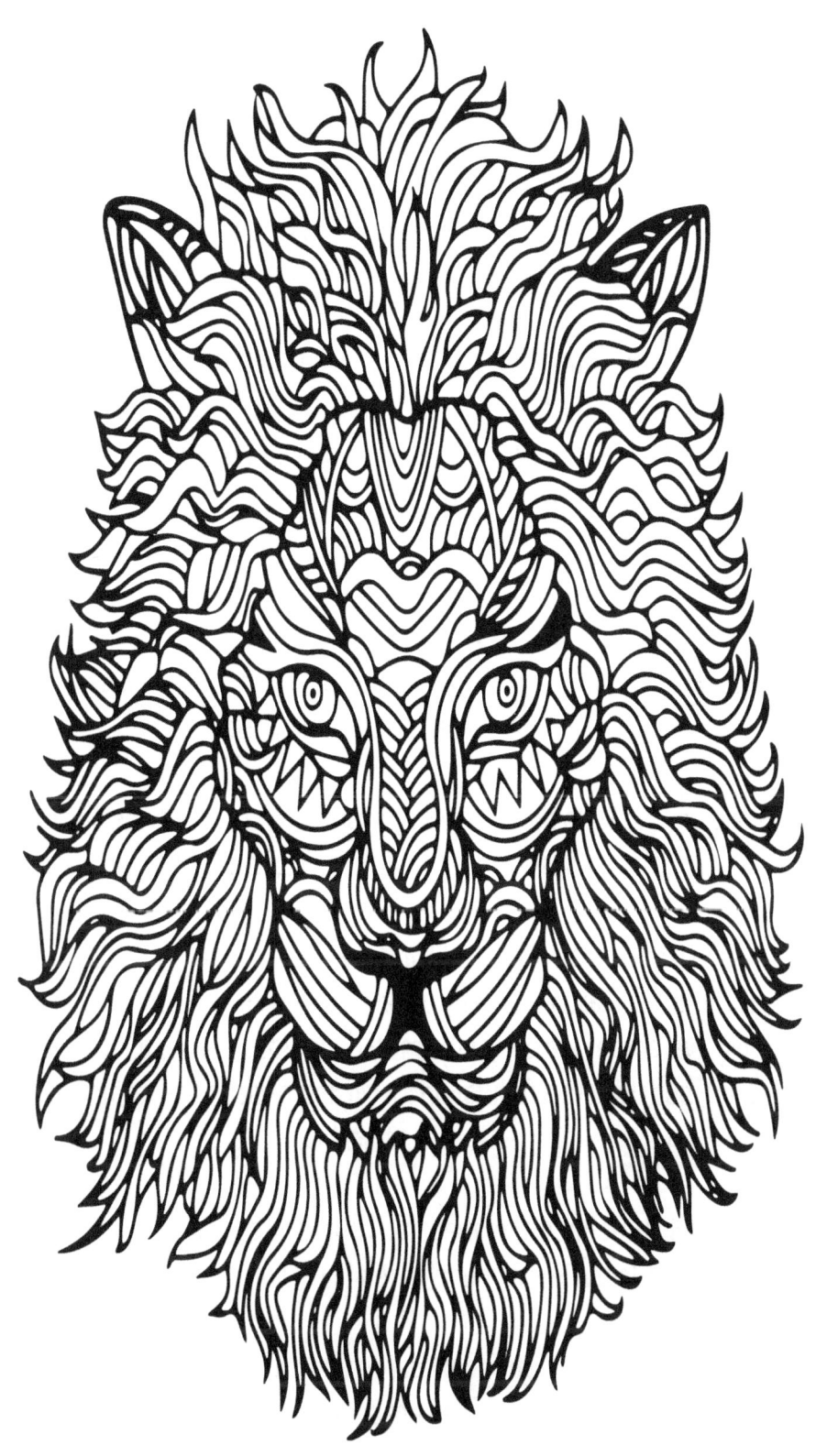

Characterised by their size and unique horns, the Cape Buffalo, also known as the Southern Savannah buffalo, is the largest of the four African buffalo sub species.

Cape buffalos are found in several east African countries, and their habitats span as far south as South Africa. Numbering at over 670,000, the majority of the population today live in protected areas, where hunting is limited and strictly controlled. Despite living in these protected areas, poaching continues to be a problem, as these buffalos are prized for their meat as well as their horns.

Although they are listed as being a species of "Least Concern" by the IUCN Red List, they have experienced sharp declines in their population in the past, largely due to poaching, habitat loss and natural diseases.

Cape buffalo are known to be the most aggresive of the sub species. They have been known to show aggression even to African elephants, lions and humans.

The African buffalo are known to kill more hunters in Africa than any other wildlife animal. This is the reason that early trophy hunters included the African buffalo, as one of the big five, as they are one of the most dangerous species to hunt. When hunted by humans, buffalo have a reputation for circling back on their attackers and counter attacking.

Lions are their most important predators, but spotted hyenas have also taken them as food. In the Suvati, buffalo are 41% of lion kills in the dry season.

The buffalo is certainly a strong presence upon the African plains, and conseravtion and protection from poachers should keep it that way.

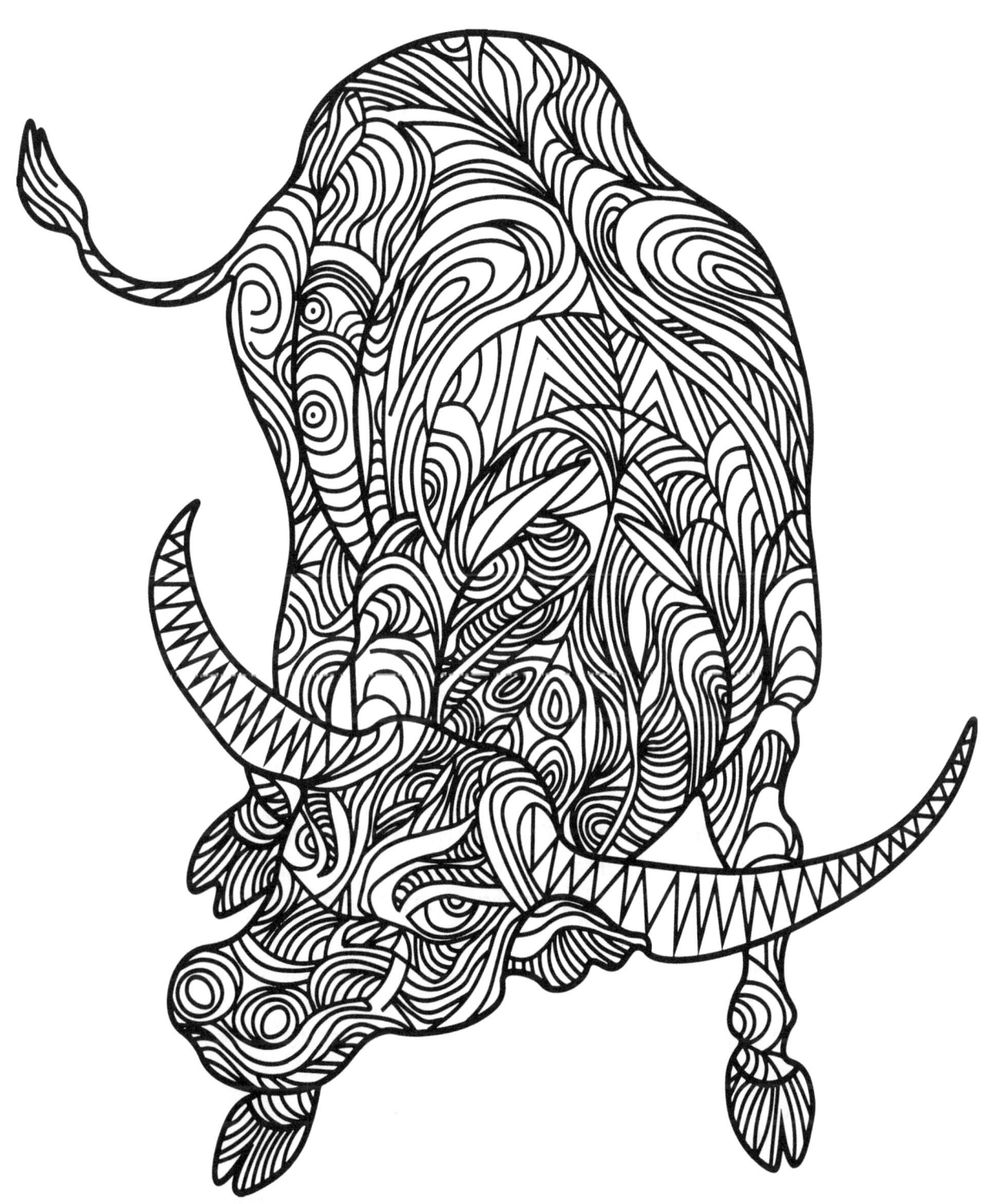

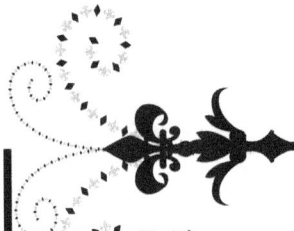

Neither graceful or beautiful, warthogs are nonetheless remarkable animals. They are found in moist and arid Savannas and can survive for months without water.

Human and wildlife conflict poses a threat to warthogs. They are killed for raiding wheat, rice, bean or groundnut fields. In some agricultural areas, people are also eliminating warthogs, as they can potentially carry African swine fever.

We need to create more protected spaces. African Wildlife Foundation works with governments and local communities , to designate wildlife corridors-large swarths of land that warthogs and other wildlife can use to roam from one park or country to another.

Lions and leopards are the warthogs main predators. They protect themselves by fleeing or sliding backwards into a hole, thus being in a position to use their formidible tusks in an attack.

The warthog has poor vision, but its senses of smell and hearing are good. When alarmed, the warthog grunts or snorts, lowers its mane, flattens its ears and bolts for underground cover.

The warthog is mainly a grazer and has adapted an interesting practice of kneeling on its calloused, hairy, padded knees to eat short grass. Using its snout and tusks, it digs for bulbs, tubers and roots during the dry season.

Before giving birth to a new litter, the female chases away the litter she has been raising and secludes hrself. These juveniles may join up with another solitary female for a short time before they go on their own.

Males weigh between 20 to 50 pounds more than females, but both are distinguished by dispproportionately large heads and warts. The face is fairly flat and the snout elongated. Eyes set high on the head enables the warthog to keep a look out for predators, when it lowers its head to feed on short grass.

They are at home on the African savanna and always are a welcome sight.

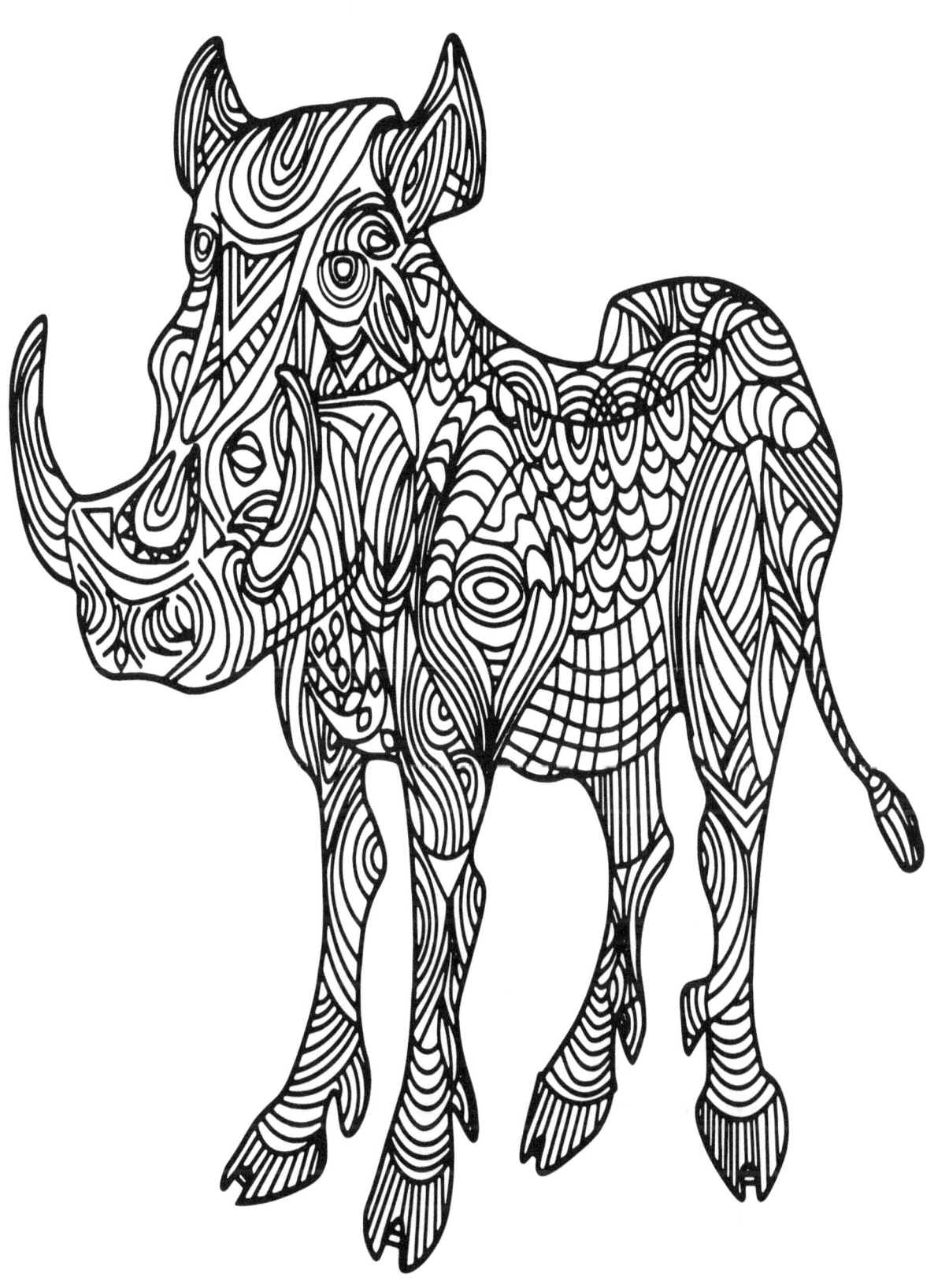

The giraffe is one of the most beautiful and calming animals that I have ever seen, and they have always been a prominent feature of Africa. Yet, the shocking truth is that some giraffes are in danger of extinction!

There are now fewer than 80,000 giraffes in Africa, 60,000 less than the 140,000 recorded 15 years ago. Two of the the nine giraffe sub species are now on the endangered red list. This is due mainly to poachers and bush meat hunters.

Wild giraffes are an easy target to poachers as they are easy to kill. Some hunters prize the giraffes head and bones as a cure for aids, even though such notions are known as nonsence in the western world.

Traditionally, some get caught in snares by poorer local people just looking for food. However, poachers hunting higher profile animals have the firearms and and automatic weapons which make it simple to kill the noticeable giraffe.

Their prominence in zoos has diguised the fact that there is very little conservation effort made with them. Thankfully, this is about to change, as we discover just how dramatically they have declined over the years. A small proportion of their demise is also due to the decline of their natural habitat, but mostly it is the poaching which is the biggest problem.

The most endangered sub species is the West African giraffe. The Giraffe Conservation Foundation estimates that only 300 remain on the whole continent.

Unless something is done soon, we could lose these glorious creatures.

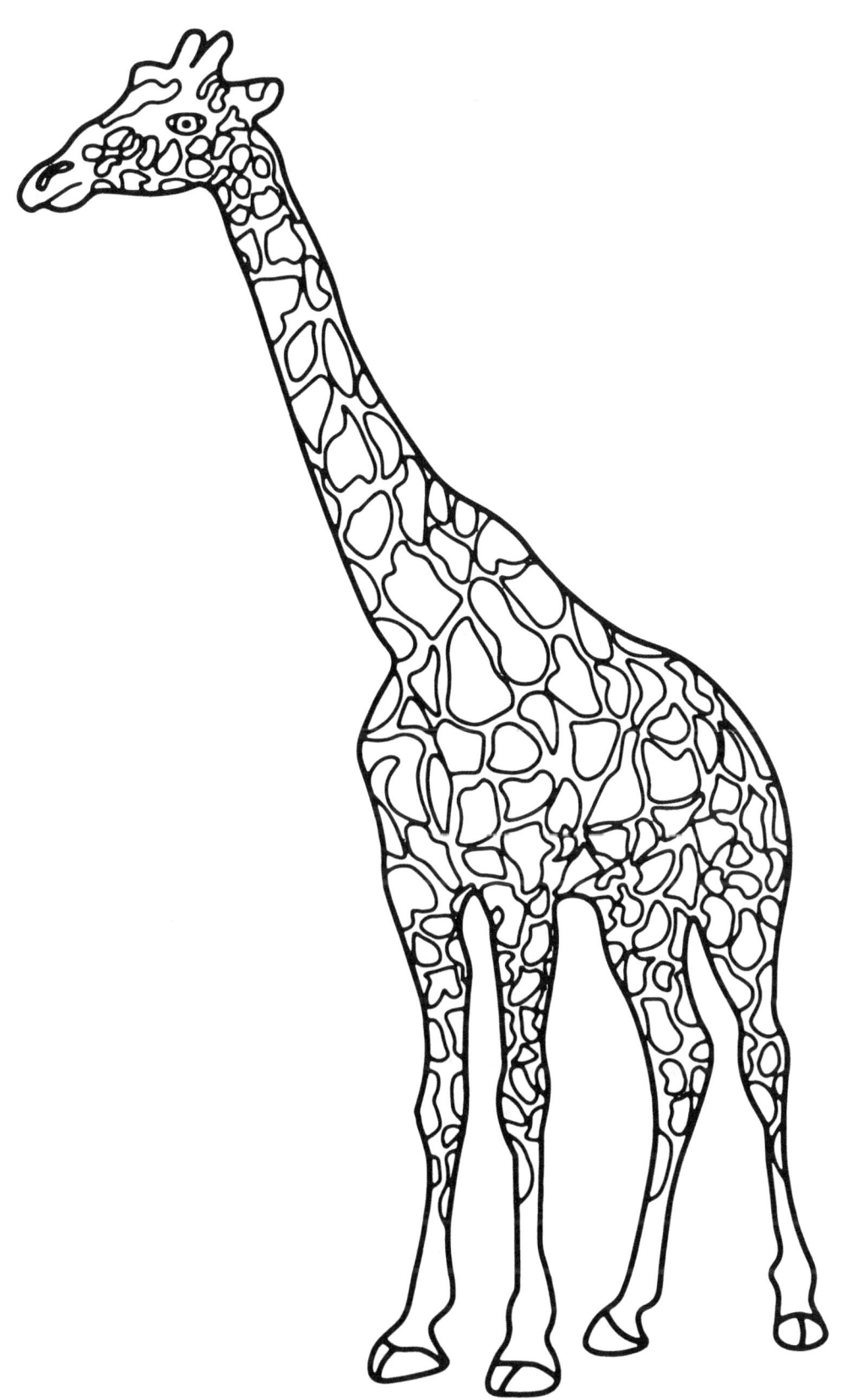

The Thompson's gazelle is just one in over 19 species of gazelles, that can be found in Africa. This gazelle inhabitats the southern parts of Kenya, and the northern parts of Tanzania. It lives on the open plains and grasslands, and is a familiar sight on the Savanna.

People hunt gazelles because of their horns, which are considered a trophy. Luckily, the number of gazelles in the wild are stable, and they are not enlisted as endangered animals.

These grazing antelopes live in herds, which can consist of as few as ten, or as many as several hundred animals. During the rainy season, thousands of animals can be seen gathering in large groups.

The gazelle is especially alert to sounds and movements, and its fine senses of hearing, sight, and smell, balance its vunerability on the open plains.

Cheetahs, lions, leopards, hunting dogs and hyenas prey on young and adults alike, with adult males three times more suscepical than females. The young are also taken by serval cats, jackals, baboons, eagles and pythons.

Thompson's gazelle breed twice a year. Although births occur throughout the year, they peak right after the rainy seaon. After giving birth, the mother hides the newborn in the grass, returning several times a day to nurse it. With their tawny colouring and their ability to remain motionless for long periods, the young are surprisingly invisible when hidden on the open plains.

The gazelles migrate towards the better sources of food and water during the dry season. During migration, they often mix with animals of other species, such as wildebeest, Grant's gazelle and zebras.

When faced with danger, the gazelle can run 40 miles per hour. While running, the gazelle occasionally jumps in the air with all four feet above the ground.

Graceful, beautiful, and elegant, these wonderful creatures bless the savanna with their presence.

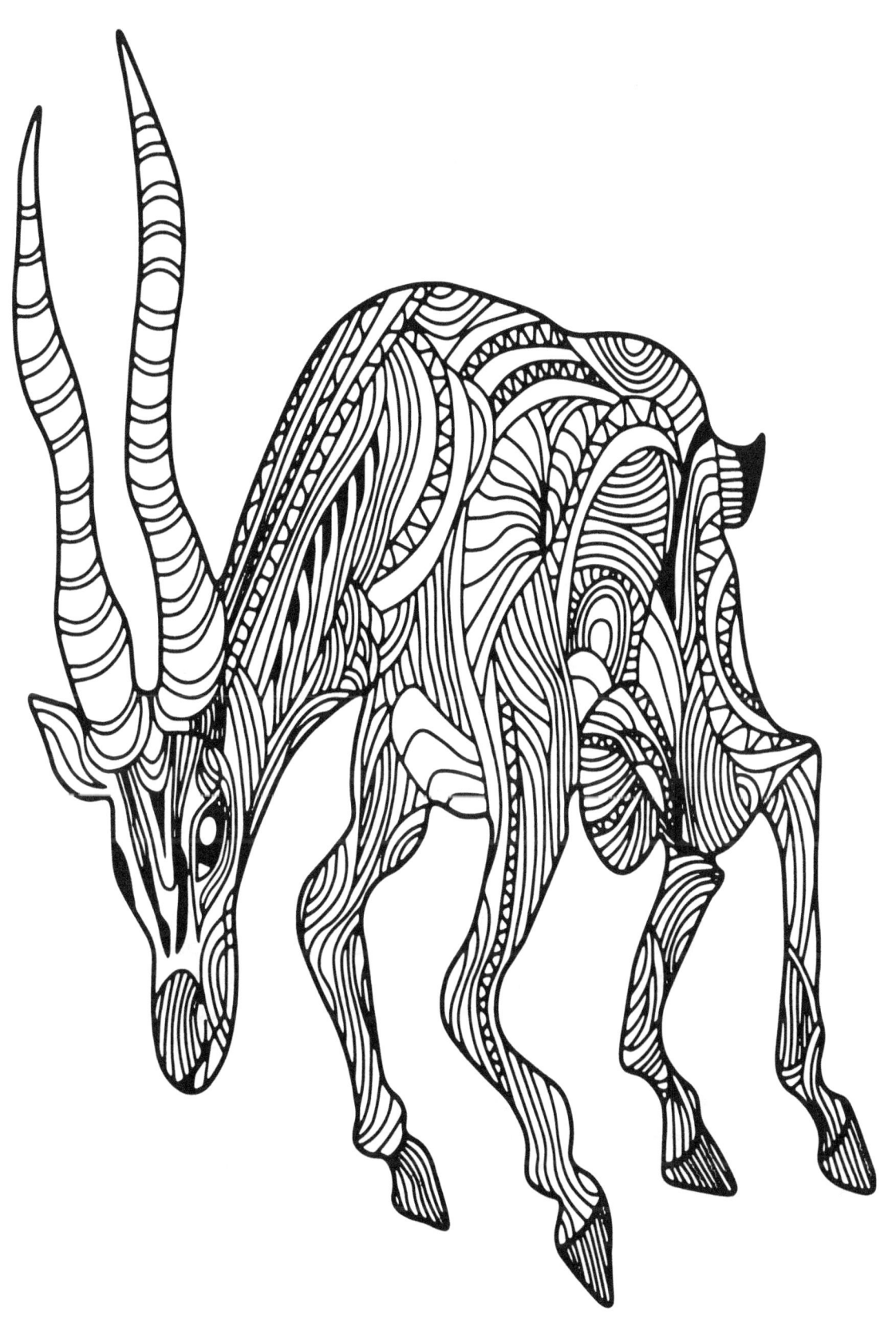

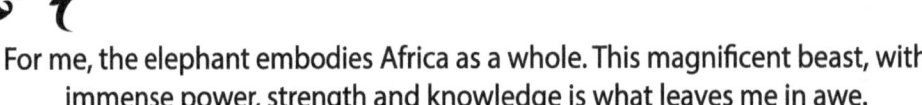

For me, the elephant embodies Africa as a whole. This magnificent beast, with immense power, strength and knowledge is what leaves me in awe.

We all know the battle this animal has faced with poaching over the years, but things are not getting any better, in fact, things are getting much worse for this majestic animal.

It is a familiar cause, but never before has it been more urgent. Last year, tens of thousands of Africa's elephants were killed to supply illegal ivory to markets throughout the world. Increasingly, revenue generated from this blood ivory, is being used to fuel war and terroism in Africa.

Animal rights groups esimate, that poachers in Africa kill between 25,000 and 35,000 elephants annually, meaning 104 elephants are being killed every single day!

Elephant numbers have dropped by 62% over the last decade, and they could be extinct by the end of the next decade. An insatiable lust for ivory products in Asian markets, makes the illegal ivory trade extremely profitable.

Elephants are a keystone species. This means that they create and maintain the ecosystems in which they live, and make it possible for the myraid of a plant and animal species to live in those environments as well.

We can save elephants by implementing stronger protection for wild elephants at both local and international levels of government; stronger enforecement and legislative measures taken against poaching and the illegal trade of ivory. Also, better management of natural elephant habitats and education, are just a few simple things to start with.

Elephants are running out of space and time. Before we know it, they will be gone, unless we collectively stop the senseless poaching and consumer demand for ivory, and allocate protected natural habiatat, in countries where elephants and other wildlife can thrive now, and in the future.

Without elephants, just what kind of world would it be?

-

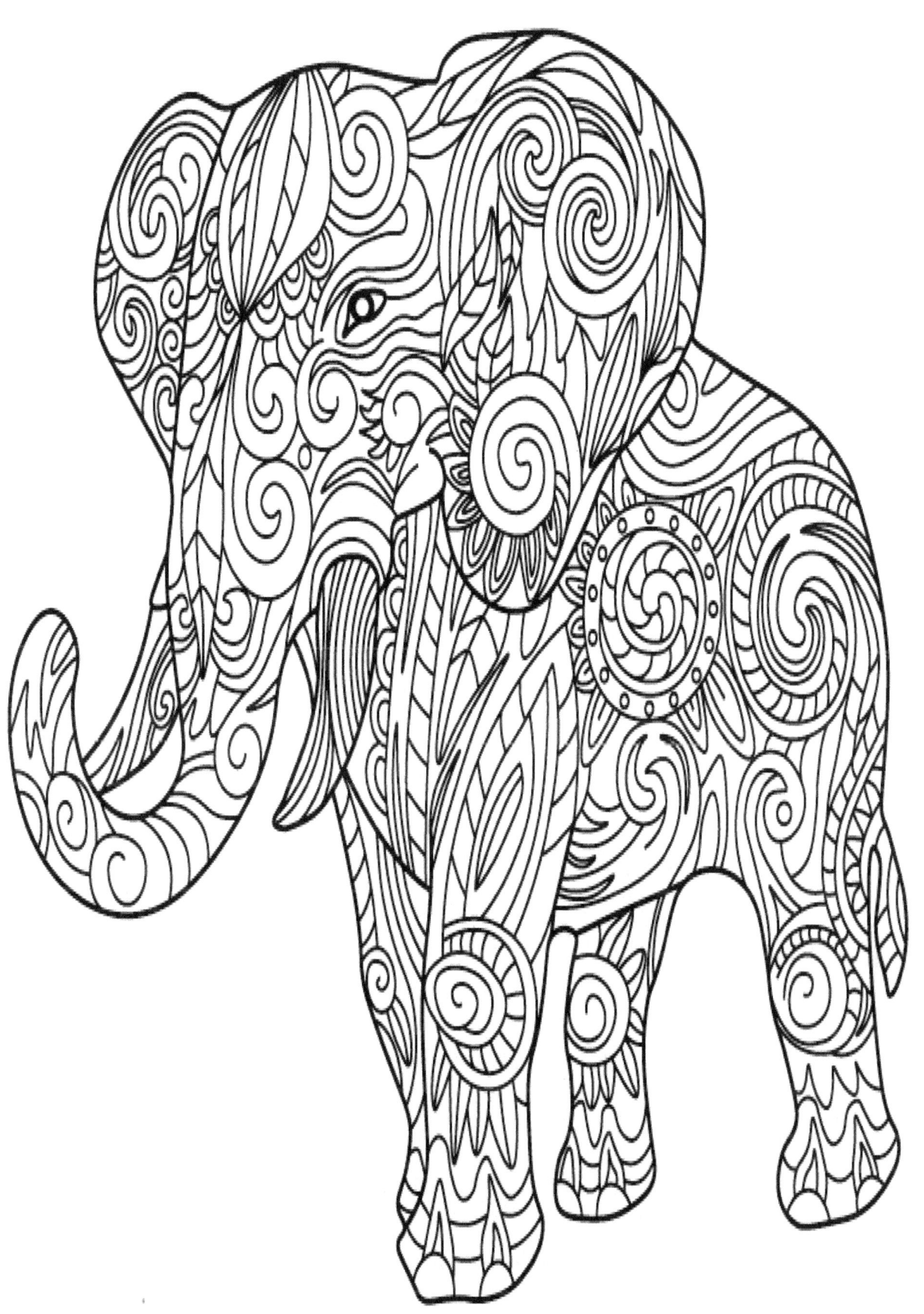

The Black Mamba, is one of Africa's largest venomous snakes, reaching an average of 2.5 metres(8 feet) in length. The biggest ones, however, can get as long as 4.5 metres (14 feet). It is also the continent's most feared snake.

Black mamba snakes live primarily in scrubland, and can also live in bushes and small trees. It is extremely aggressive, and will not hesitate to strike. Fast and agile, it can reach speeds of up to 12mph.

Despite its name the "black" mamba, it is not black but rather brown/olive or brownish grey in colour. The snake has an inky black mouth, which is displayed when threatened.

The Black Mamba has an extremely potent neuro and cardio-toxic venom, capable of killing a dozen men in as little as an hour. Without anti-venom, the mortality rate from a Black Mamba bite is almost 100%.

Diet-wise, it feeds on creatures such as moles, rats, mice, birds and other small mammels.

Breeding usually takes place in the late spring or early summer. The female will lay between 10 and 25 eggs, usually in decaying vegetation. Hatchlings are independant immediately, and can catch prey the size of a small rat.

Young Black Mambas are preyed upon by mongooses, and adult Black Mambas are eaten by the secretary bird and larger species of eagle.

The stunning 'Black Mamba's', are also the first all female anti-poaching unit, risking their lives to protect big cats, rhinos and elephants from man in Africa.

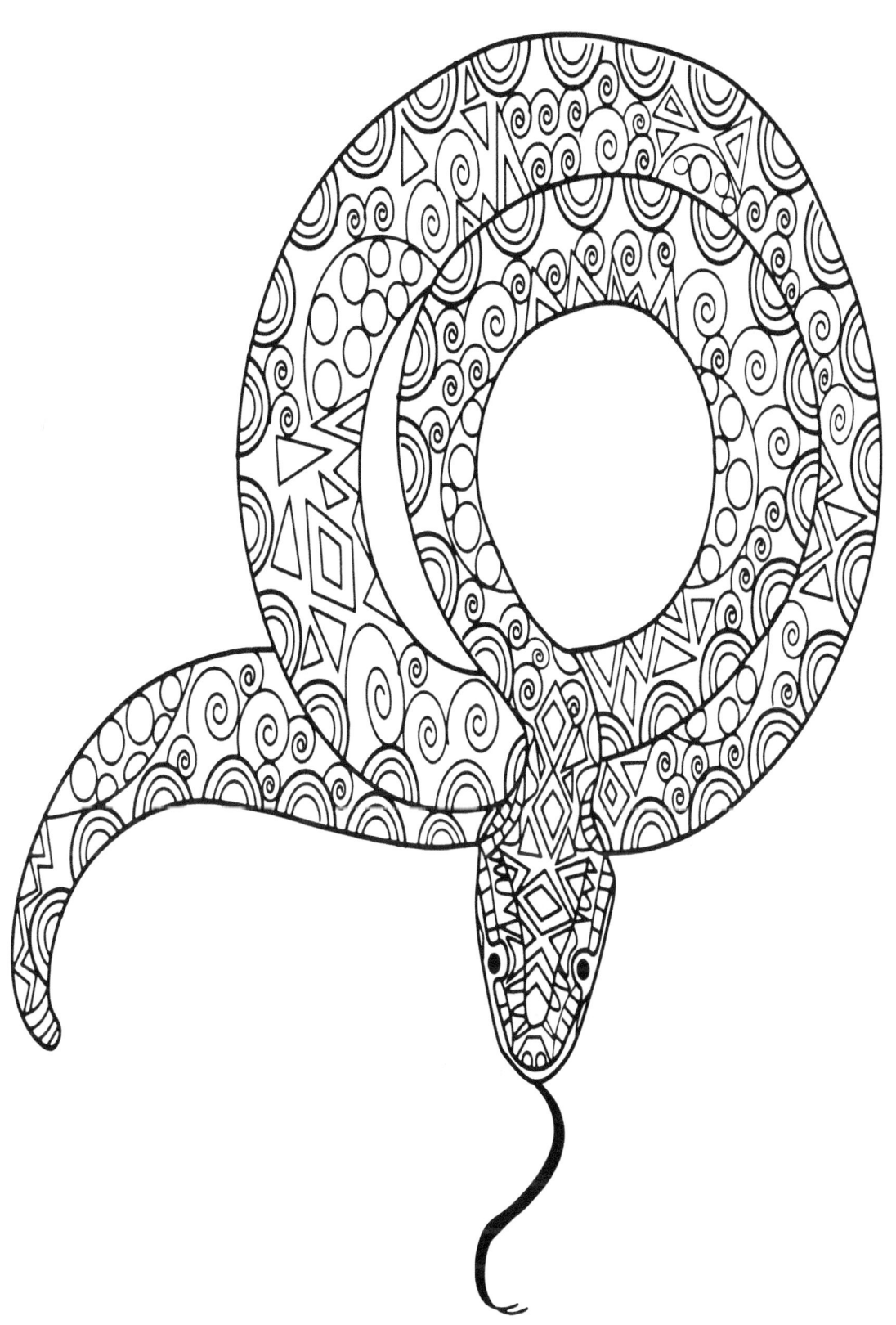

Rhino poaching is currently at crisis point! By the end of 2015, the number of African rhinos killed by poachers had increased for the 6th year in a row, with at least 1338 rhinos killed by poachers across Africa in 2015.

South Africa has by far, the largest population of rhinos in the world, and is an incredibily importatnt country for rhino conservation. However, rhino poaching levels have drastically escalated over recent years.

Worringly, the crisis has spread to neighbouring countries in southern Africa, with Namibia and Zimbabwe experiencing a potential increase in poaching. For Africa as a whole, the total number of rhinos poached during 2015 was the highest in two decades.

Rhinos were once abundant in Africa and Asia, with an approximated population of 500,000 in the early twentieth century. However, despite intensive conservation efforts, poaching of this iconic species is dramatically increasing, pushing the remaining rhinos closer and closer to extinction.

The Western black rhino was declared extinct by the IUCN in 2011, with the primary cause identified as poaching. In fact, all five remaining rhino species are listed on the IUCN Redlist of threatened species, with three out of five species classified as criticaly endangered.

The current poaching crisis is attributed to the growing demand for rhino horn in Asian countries, mainly Vietnam and China. Vietnam has been identified as the largest user of rhino horn. Although rhino horn has no scientific medical benefits, consumers are using it to treat a wide range of conditions, from cancer to hangovers, and due to its high value, it is now also used as a status by wealthy individuals.

The high price fetched for the horn has attracted the involvement of ruthless criminal syndicates, who use high-tech equiptment to track down and kill the rhinos.

Law enforcement plays a crucial role in deterring poachers, however, there is no simple answer to combat the current poaching crisis. A variey of strategies are needed to combat poaching including rigorous anti-poaching and monitering patrols, community conservation and environmental education schemes, captive breeding, translocations and demand reduction in Asia.

These wonderful beasts are without a doubt the most endangered animal in the world, and we must fight to save them before any more sub-species become extinct like the Western black rhino.

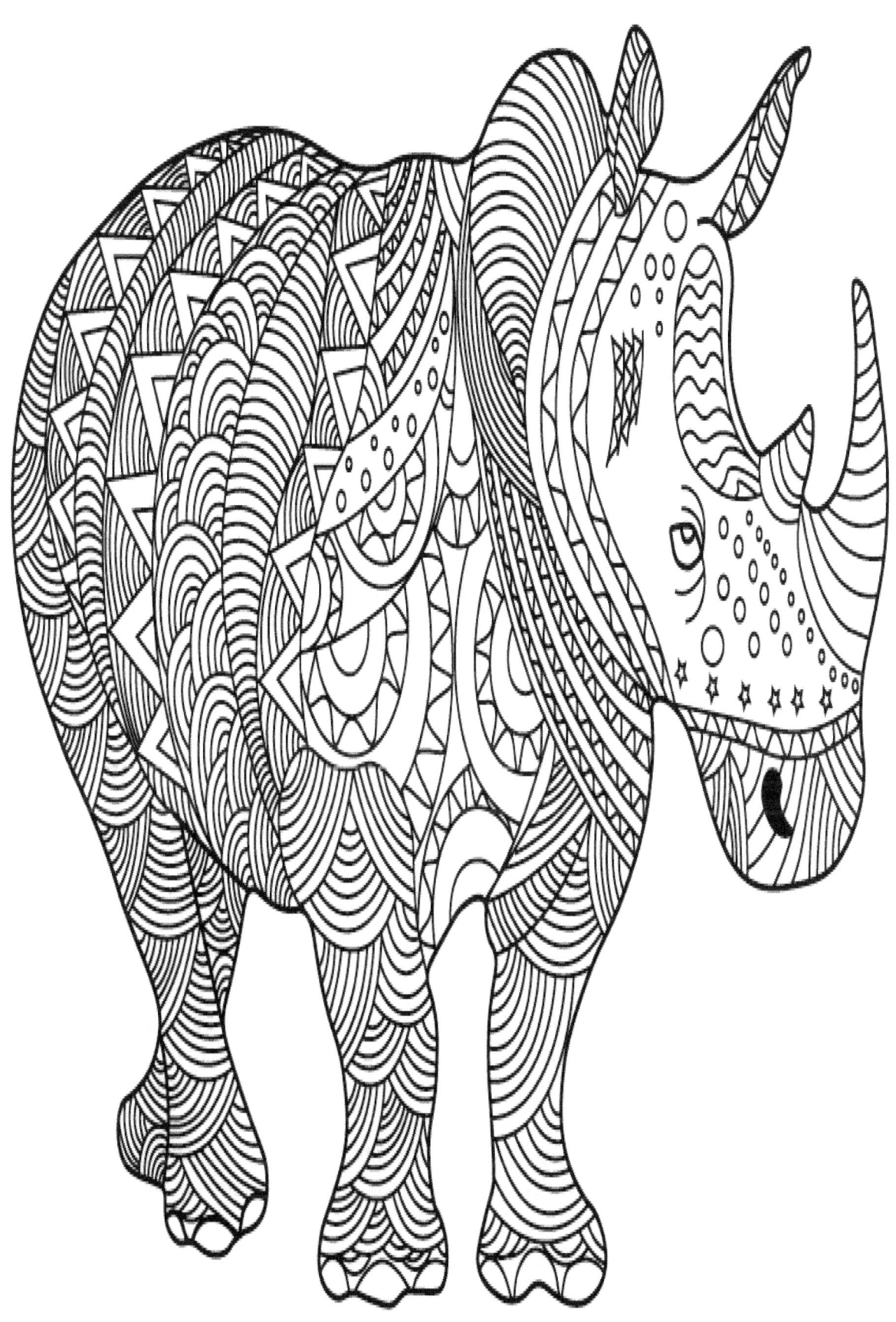

The cheetah is best known for being the fastest animal on the planet. They live in grasslands, savannas, and semi-arid areas that have enough open space and plenty of prey. The biggest popualtion of cheetah is found in Africa, and cheetahs can also be found in Asia. Both groups are endangered, especially the Asian type, with only 250 remaining in the wild.

The cheetah is easily recognised by its orange fur and black spots, it has two black lines called black tears, which run from the inside of their eyes. Scientists believe that this protects the cheetah's eye from a harsh African sun, and helps them to see long distance.

The cheetah hunts different animals: warthogs, rabbits, gazelles, antelopes, impalas, porcupines, spring hares and even ostriches.

The cheetah's tail is essential during fast running, it balances the animal, and allows fast and sudden turns. After 400 to 600 yards, the cheetah becomes exhausted and needs to take a rest. Unlike most other cats, the cheetah is not a good tree climber, and it is the only big cat that cannot roar.

The cheetah's future is uncertain due to a variety of threats. The biggest is habitat loss due to human encroachment and poaching. In addition, they often deal with declines in prey and conflicts with humans. There is also high cub mortality due to carnivores like the lion. Hyenas that are in competition with the cheetah, as well as genetic inbreeding, which leads to abnormalities.

The cheetah's future may look dim, but conservationists have been working to lesson the decline in some areas. In the early 1990's, conservationists began educating livestock farmers around Namibia about how to reduce cheetah/livestock interactions, and teaching farmers how to avoid conflict through breeding schedueles, and the use of guard dogs to protect livestock as alternatives to resorting to the rifle.

These efforts, along with stronger enforcement of endangered species, and anti-poaching laws, have resulted in stabilized populations in that country.

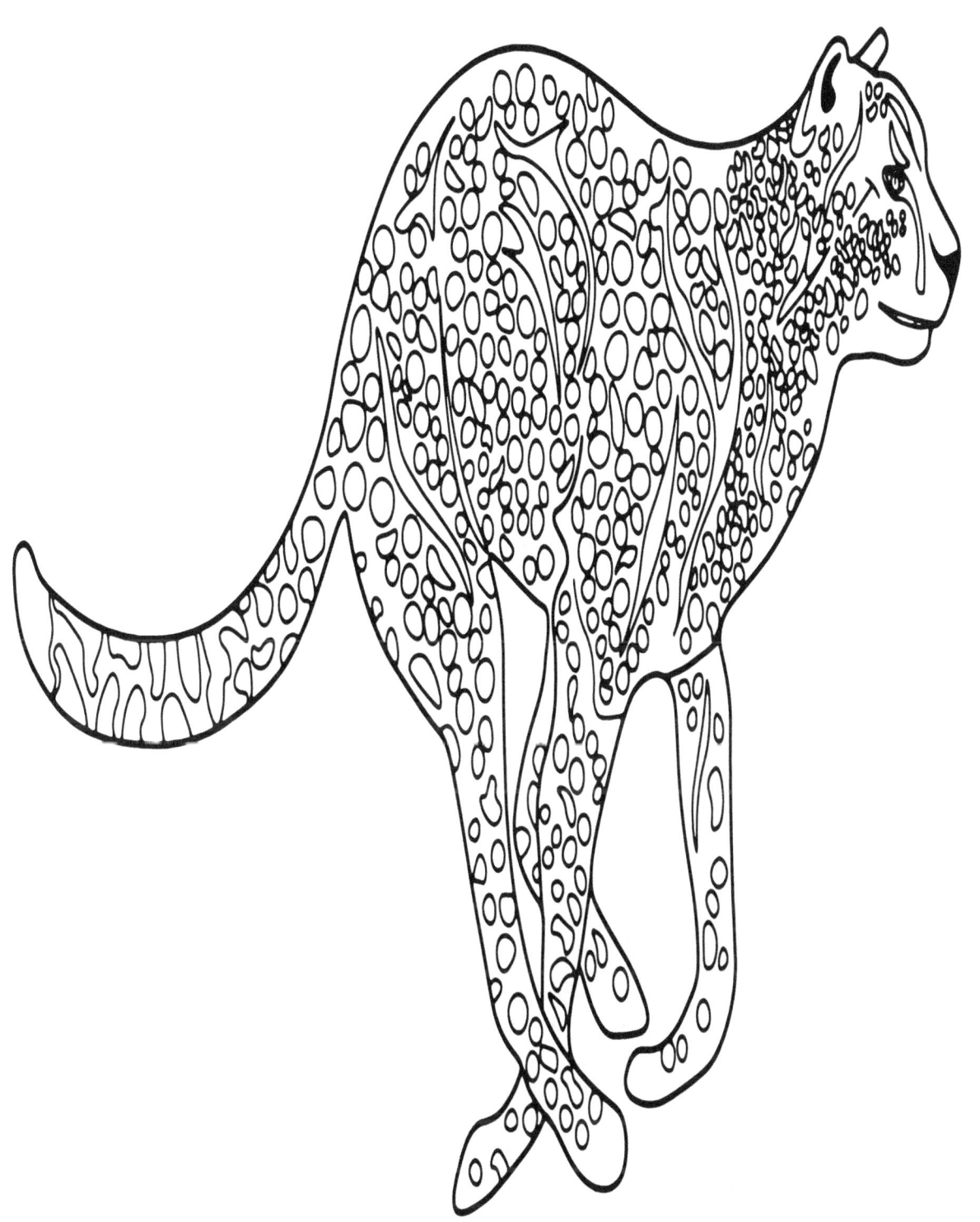

Considerable variations exist throughout the range of the Nile crocodie. Generally, it is a large crocodilian, averaging at 5 metres in length, but reportedly reaching 6 metres in some instances. Juveniles are dark olive-brown, with black cross banding on the tail and body, this banding becomes fainter in adults.

A fully grown adult can take a wide range of large vertebrates, including antelope, buffalo, young hippos and large cats. Fish and smaller vertebrates often form the greatest part of their diet, however, they have a reputation as man-eaters, they have killed more people than all of the other crocodilian species combined.

Nile crocodiles will also scavange carcasses, together with a number of other animals, all of which seem to tolerate each other's presence. Several prey animals have been found wedged under submerged branches and stones, leading to reports that crocodiles store unwanted prey until a later date.

Social behaviour in Nile crocodiles is often underestimated, and there are many aspects still poorly understood. It has been observed, that social status may influence an individuals feeding success, with less dominant animals tending to eat less in situations where they come into frequent social contact with other, more dominant individuals.

This species digs hole nests up to 50cm deep, in sandy banks, several metres from water. These may be in close proximity to other nests. Both males and females have been reported to assist hatching, by gently cracking open eggs between their tounge and upper palette. Despite the vigilance of the female during the incubation period, a high percentage of nests are raided by other animals, from hyenas, to moniter lizards and humans.

In the 1940's through to the 1960's, this crocodile was hunted close to extinction. Local and international protections have helped them rebound in most areas. In some regions, due to pollution, hunting, and habitat loss, their numbers are still severely depleted.

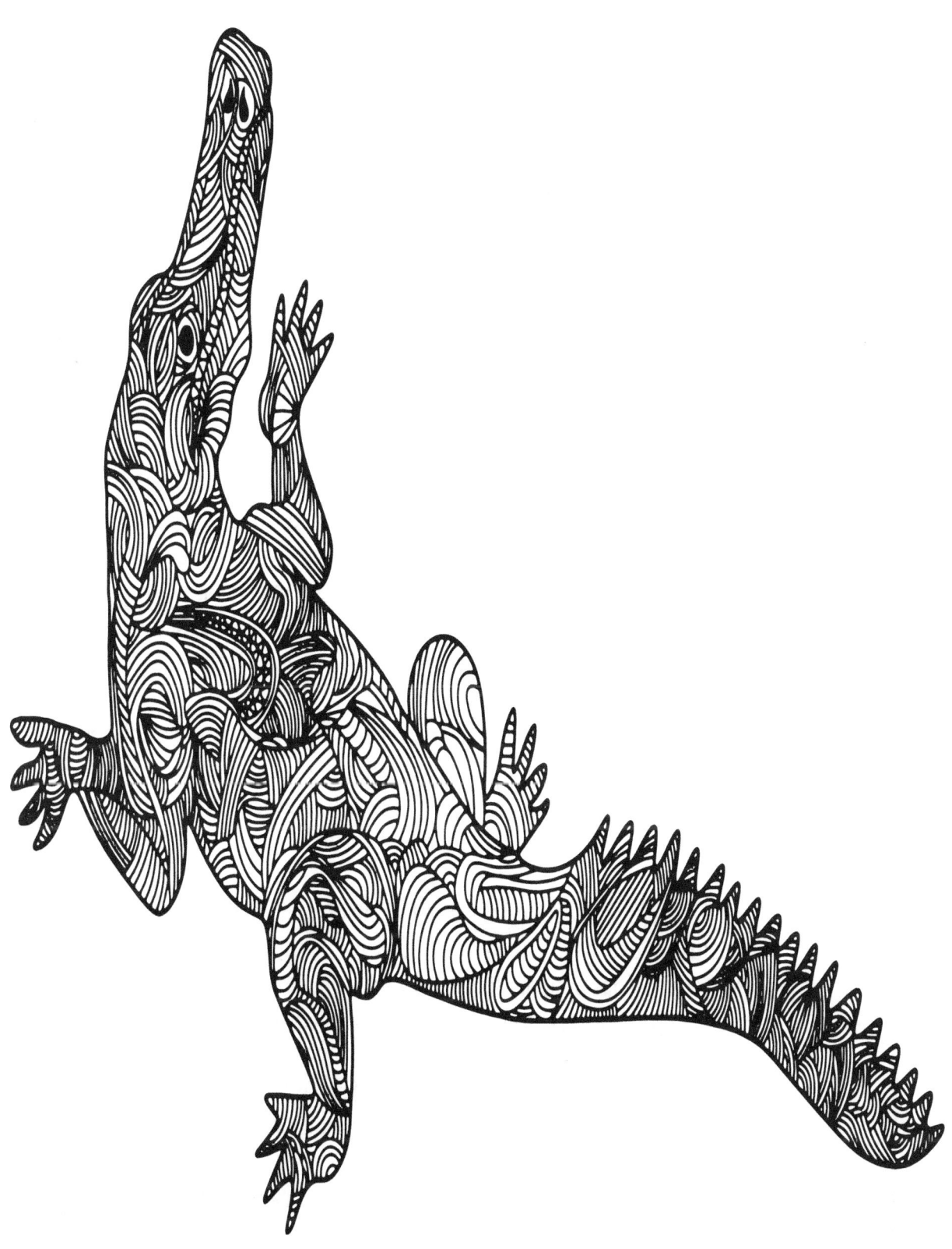

Zebras have horse-like bodies, but their manes are made of short, erect hair, their tails are tufted at the tip, and their coats are striped. There are three species of zebra in Africa, two of which are found in East Africa. The most numerous and widespread species in the east, is Burchell's, also known as the plains zebra. The other is Grevy's zebra, named after Jules Grevy, a president of France in the 1880's, who recieved one Abyssinia as a gift, and now is mostly found in northern Kenya. The third species is the mountain zebra is found in southern and south-western Africa.

Zebras have shiny coats and dissipate over 70 per cent of incoming heat, some scientists believe the stripes help the animals withstand solar radiation. The black and white stripes are a form of camouflage called disruptive colourtaion, which breaks up the outline of the body. Although the pattern is visible during the daytime, at dawn or in the evening when their predators are most active, zebras look indistinct and may confuse predators by distorting true distance.

Burchell's zebras inhabit savannas, from treeless grasslands to open woodlands: they sometimes occur in tens of thousands in migratory herds on the Serengeti plains. Some zebras have been known to compete with livestock for water and have suffered heavy poaching for their meat and skins.

Family groups are stable members and maintain strong bonds over many years. Mutual grooming helps develop and preserve these bonds. They look out for one another, and if one becomes separated from the rest, the others will search for it. The group adjusts its travelling pace to accomodate the old and the weak.

They are avid grazers and are in constant search of green pastures. In the dry season, they can live on coarse, dry grass if they are near water.

A zebras main predators are lions and hyenas, and to a lesser extent hunting dogs, leopards and cheetahs. When a family group is attacked, they form a semicircle, face the predator and watch it, ready to bite or strike should the attack continue.

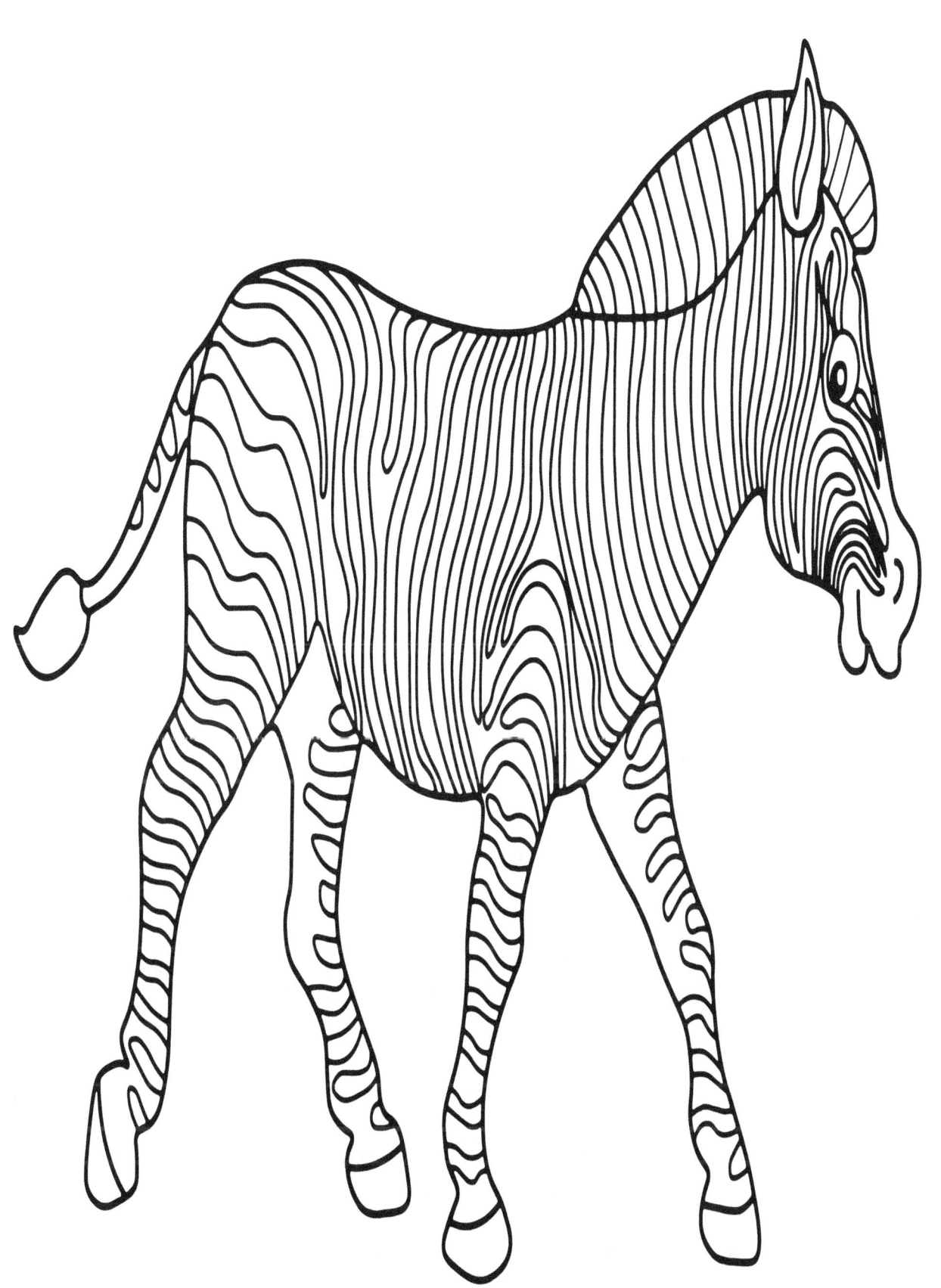

Chimpanzees have already disappeared from four African countries, and are nearing extinction in many others. Deforestation and commercial hunting for bushmeat are taking a terrible toll on most populations.

Disease can also play a major factor in the dramtic loss of numbers. In late 2002, an outbreak of Ebola hemorrhagic fever in humans, was reported in the north of the Republic of Congo on the border with Gabon. The human infections coincided with a large scale wipe out of great apes in the region. Two great apes found in Central Africa, the area currently affected by Ebola: Western Lowland Gorilla and the Central Chimpanzee. Both have been severly affected by the virus, which has drastically reduced populations

Chimpanzees are one of our closest relatives, sharing an estimated 98% of their genes with humans. Four sub-species have been identified, based on differences in appearence and distribution. There is a wide range of differences between groups from different regions, so the loss of any one group represents a loss of cultural as well as biological heritage.

Chimpanzees are found in savanna woodlands, grassland forest mosaics, from sea level to about 3000m in elevation. Chimpanzees are highly social animals, their communities consist of loose and flexible males and females within a mixed home range, led by a dominant male. Members join and leave these communities freely.

As a great ape, chimpanzees are a WWF priority species. WWF treats all priority species as one of the most ecologically, economically and culturally important species on our planet.

The WWF Great Ape Program, is working with many partners to conserve remaining populations, especially in West Africa. Their approach includes strengthening, establishing and maintaining protected areas in a number of chimpanzee range states. It aims to develop chimpanzee focused eco-tourism, and stop the illegal killing of chimpanzees, due to logging recessions and looking for solutions to stop the impact of bushmeat trade on the species.

Due to a lack of data in many regions, current estimates for the wild population range from 150,000 to 250,000 individuals. The distribution is still wide, but considerbly smaller and more fragmented.

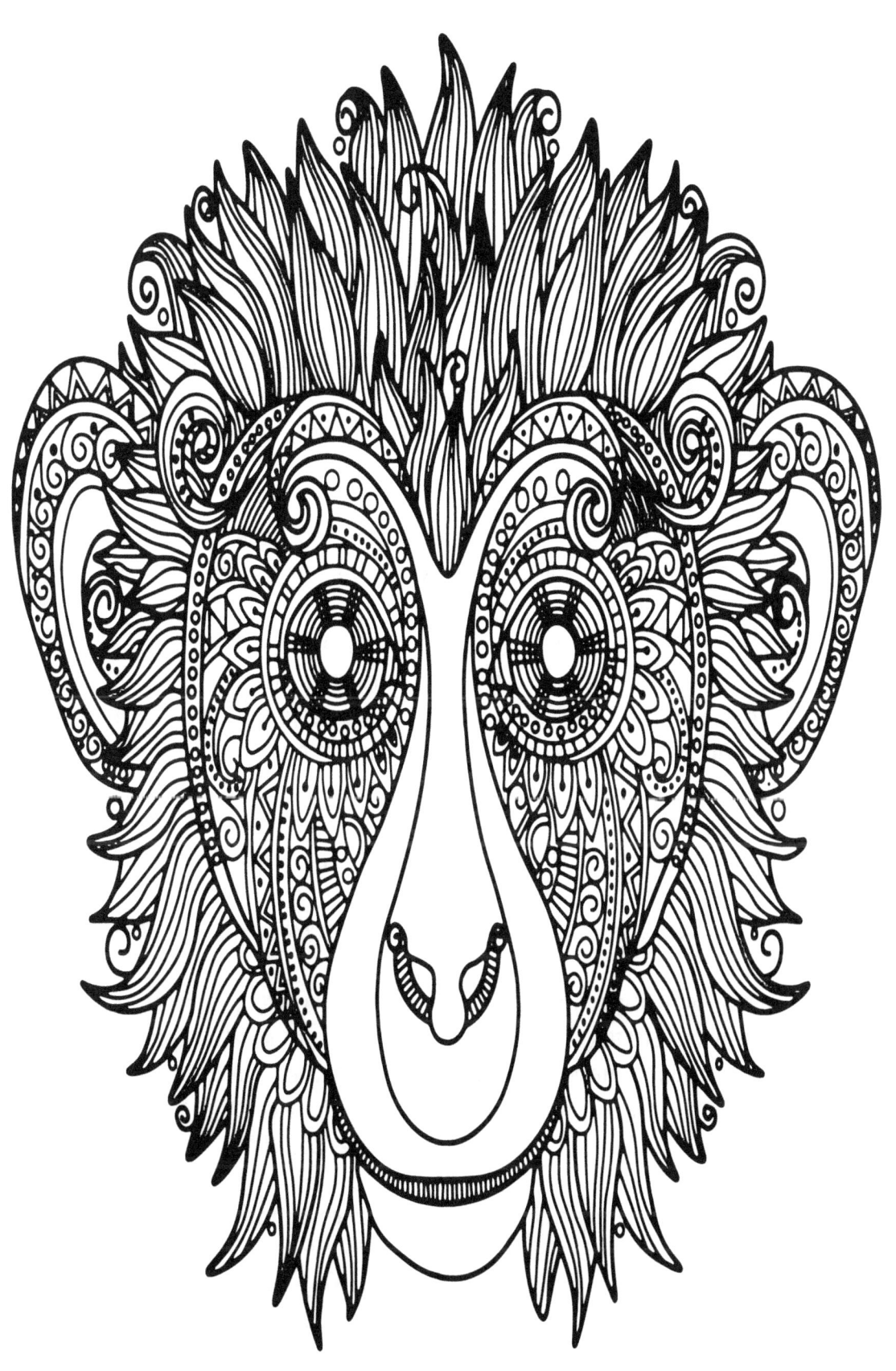

The hippo is responsible for more human fatalities in Africa, than any other large animal. Male hippos actively defend their terrotories which run along the banks of rivers and lakes. Females have also been known to get extremely aggressive if they sense anyone coming in between their babies, who stay in the water while she feeds on the shore.

Hippos can run at speeds of over 20mph, and they have enormous jaws which host up to 20 inch canines. They submit a natural sunscreen that is coloured red and eventually turns brown. Hippos can kills crocodiles and they can consume over 100 pounds of vegetation a day.

The hide of a hippo alone, can weigh half a ton, and this creature is the third largest mammel, after elephants and white rhinos. Two hippo species are found in Africa, the Large Hippo, and the Pygmy Hippo. The Large Hippo is the most aggressive of the two.

Hippos move easily in water, either swimming by kicking their hind legs, or walking on the bottom. They are well adapted to their aquatic life, with small ears, eyes and nostrils set at the top of the head. These senses are so alert, that even submerged fully in water, the hippo is alert to its surroundings. By closing its ears and nostrils, the adult can stay under water for as long as six minutes.

Amazingly agile for their bulk, hippos are good climbers and often traverse rather steep banks each night to graze on grass. They enter and exit the water at the same spots, and graze for four to five hours each night in loop patterns, covering one or two miles.

A single young is born either on land or in shallow wter. In water, the mother helps the newborn to the surface, later teaching it to swim. Newly born hippos are relatively small, weighing from 55 to 120 pounds, and are protected by their mothers, not only from crocodiles and lions, but from male hippos, who will attack them in water but not bother them on land. Scientists believe such behaviour is purely terrotorial.

Compared to other animals, hippos are not very susceptible to disease, so in suitable habitats, their numbers can increase quickly. Their primary predators are people, who may hunt hippos for their meat, hides, and ivory teeth.

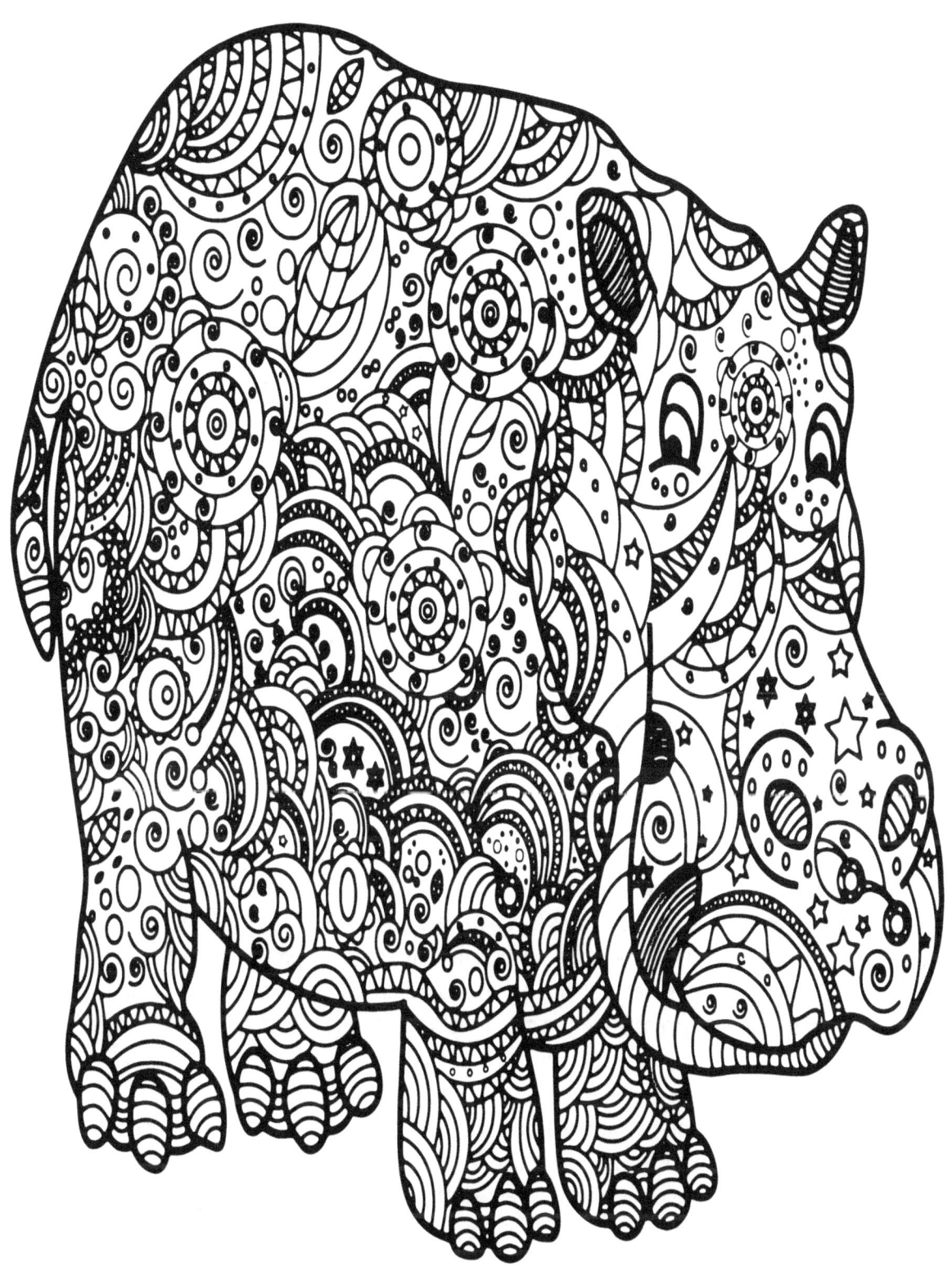

In the last thirty years, Africa's eight vulture species have declined in numbers by 62%. Six of these species are deemed as critically endangered according to recent reports. Across Africa, vultures are electrocuted by power lines or crushed by wind turbines. Witch doctors believe the brain of the vulture has magical powers, and because of this, they are hunted by poachers. Poachers also kill vultures as they are seen circling carcasses, thus alerting the authorites to a possible illegal kill. They have also been found dead after eating carcasses that been laced with pesticides intended for lions and other predators.

While vultures are not cute and cuddly, they are one of nature's most important scavengers They take years to mature and breed slowly, so it is because of this factor that with their current rate of decline, vultures may well be extinct from Africa between 50 and 100 years from now. If that happens, it would be a catastrophe as it would destroy the balance of the eco system.

The most common species of vulture found in Africa, is the African white backed vulture. It is found mostly in the northern regions of Africa, and it often inhabits the savannas, the African plains, and occasionally, it has been found in some desert regions. This species of vulture may live singly, or in colonies, but even the solitary vulture will be in close proximity to a colony most of the time.

Vultures have muscular legs, sharp talons and sharp bills. Ticks and other parasites will not stay on the neck of a vulture for long, as the neck is exposed to ultra violet rays to kill bacteria. The vulture also likes to rub its neck on rocks to clean itself. They have incredible eyesight during the day, which enables them to spot their prey while soaring in the sky. A vulture can spot a large animal carcass from around four miles away on open grassland or the savanna plains. They also have a well developed sense of smell which helps them find food.

The main predators of vultures are hawks, snakes and wild cats. In the hot African sun, the vultures have a unique way of cooling themselves by urinating. This not only cools them, but disinfects their legs which kills any germs they may have picked up walking through carcasses.

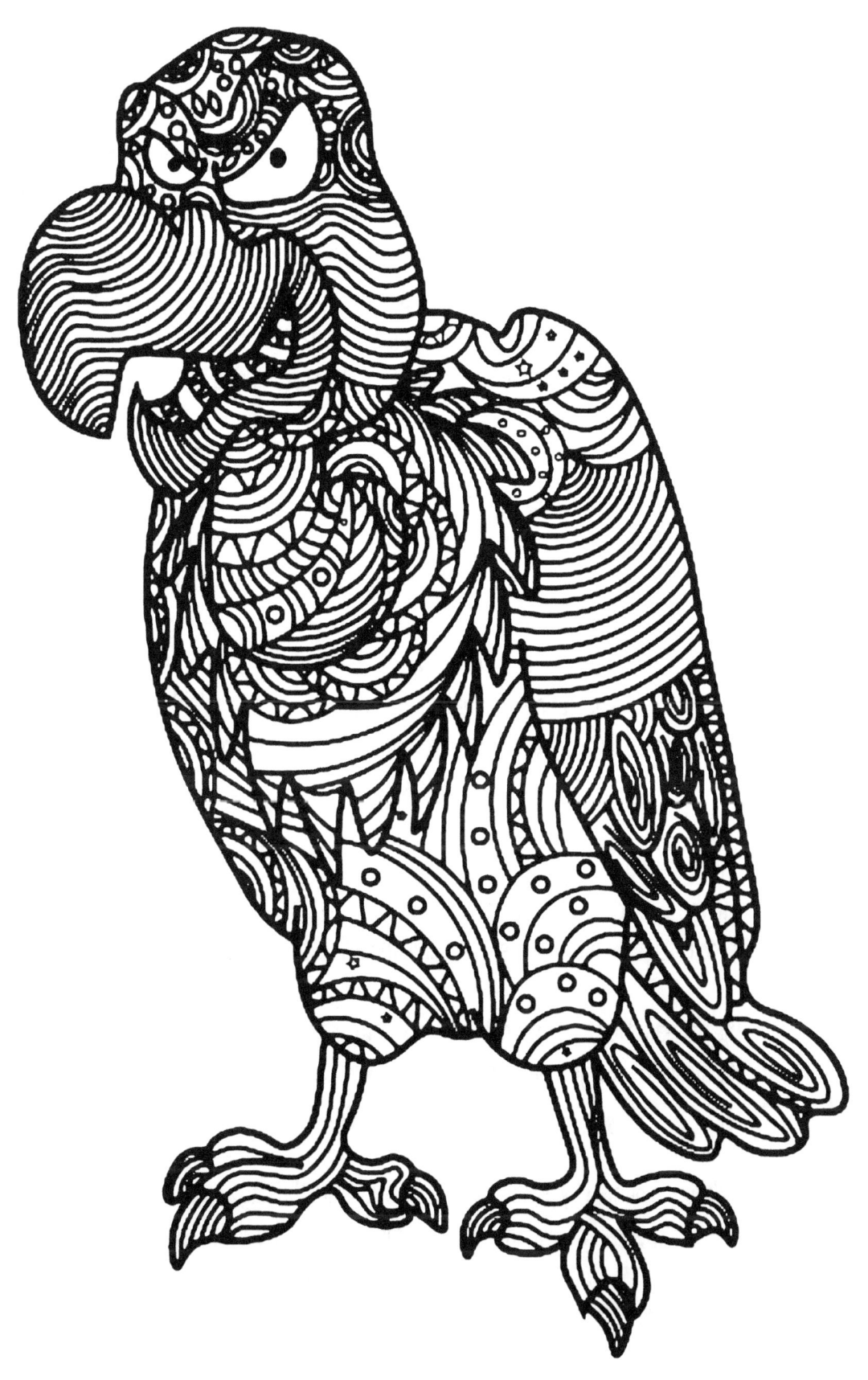

The Bat Eared Fox is one of Africa's more cuter looking animals. Named after its huge bat like ears, it can be found on the savannas and open plains near to where beetles and termites are found. Termites make up to 80% of a foxes diet as well as small rodents, lizards and birds eggs. Bat Eared Foxes are primarily nocturnal, they emerge from their underground dens at dusk to feed during the night.

Bat-eared foxes live in groups of mating pairs with their young. They are usually monogamous and breed yearly, producing litters of around six pups. These family groups social groom, play, and sleep together. The male undertakes most parental care duties, while the female forages for food to maintain her milk production.

The predators of a bat-eared fox are jackals, birds of prey, and humans. It is a known fact that bat-eared foxes are losing their habitat to humans. The African Wildlife Foundation is currently embarking on several programs, to work with local communites and with wildlife scouts so that the future of this animal in the wild is a success.

One of the most endearing habits of the bat-eared fox, is the way they walk with their ears close to the ground when foraging. They will suddenly stop, listen intently, and then dig furiously to catch their prey. Their ears are able to pick up the movements of insects underground.

The bat-eared fox has extremely pointed teeth, which enables it to quickly, and efficiently, chew its meals to aid digestion. They seldom drink water as they obtain most of the moisture which they need from their food.

Although hunted by people, their populations are thriving and so they are not classed as an endangered species. The avarage bat-eared fox, will live to be about six years old in the wild, although they can live up to thirteen years.

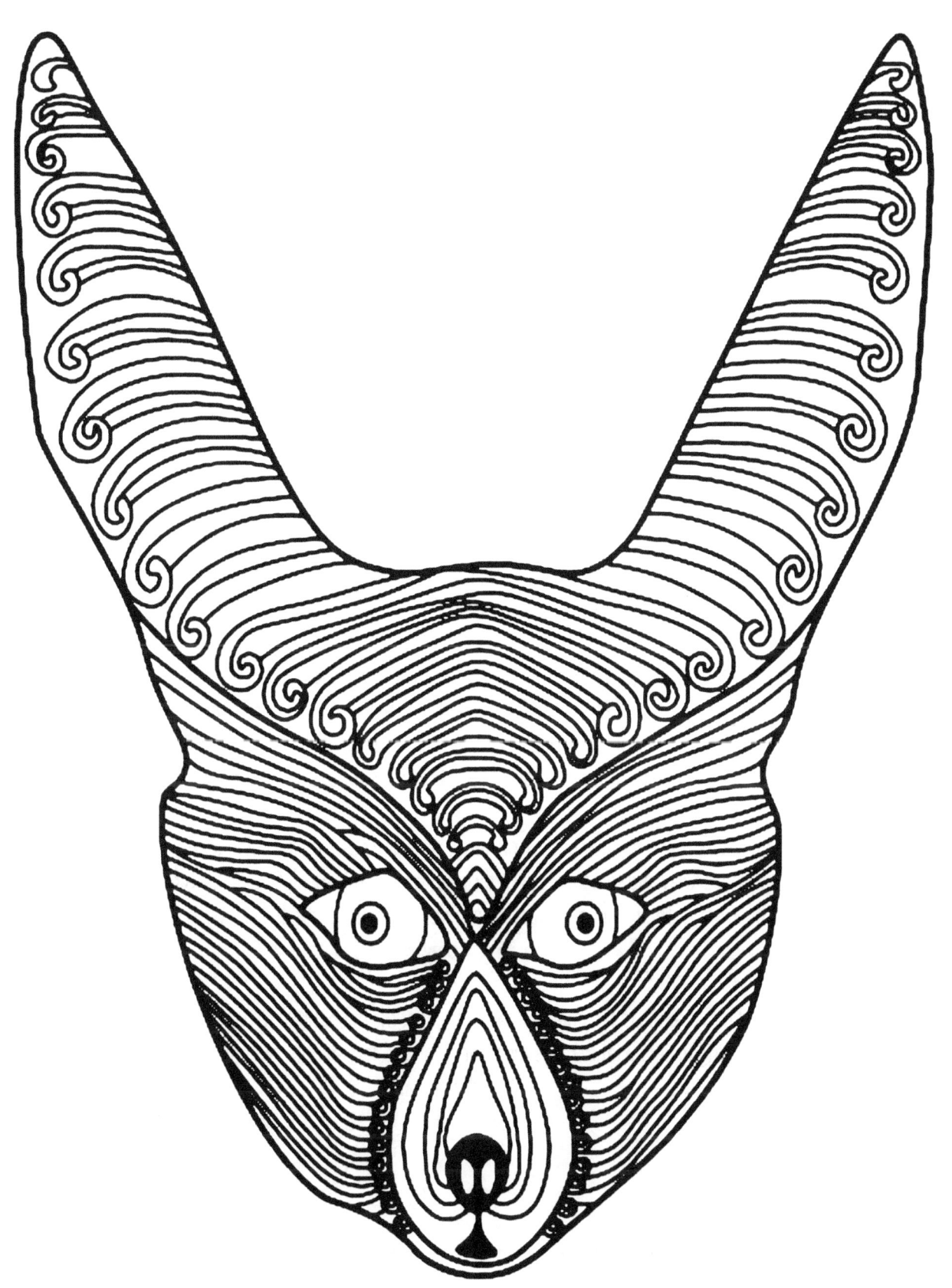

The baboon, is one primate who is constantly adapting to its ever changing surroundings, and the situations it may find itself in. They are the most widespread primates in South Africa. They are avid opportunists, with very high intelligence. The most common species is the Chacma baboon, which can be found throughout Africa.

A baboon troop is one of the most complex, subtle societies in the animal kingdom. Humans and baboon have much in common. Both are extreme generalists, able to survive on a vast variety of food, and both have a high degree of social intellegence.

Baboons are essentially omnivorous. They will eat tubers, roots, buds, sap, mushrooms, lichens, rhizomes, grasshoppers, scorpions, shellfish, lizards, nestlings, small rodents and fish. They will even kill baby antelope if they can, and they are known to scrounge and raid from humans.

Sometimes, baboons are killed when a conflict occurs between themselves and humans. This is all too common in some areas of Africa, like Cape town for instance. In 2010, such conflicts became out of control, and as a result, problem males were trapped and killed. Several years on, the problem still exists, but the removal of such males from a troop of baboons has had a detrimental effect.

Baboons have strong muscular bodies, powerful jaws, and razor sharp canine teeth. They have been known to chase away and sometimes kill attacking lions. The lifespan of a baboon is between 20 to 30 years on average. Their main predators are cheetahs, lions, leopards, hyenas, pythons and birds of prey.

With the known conflicts, it comes as no surprise, that the main threat to baboons is man. Humans are destroying their habitat to make room for crops and settlements, but, they are also hunted for their meat.

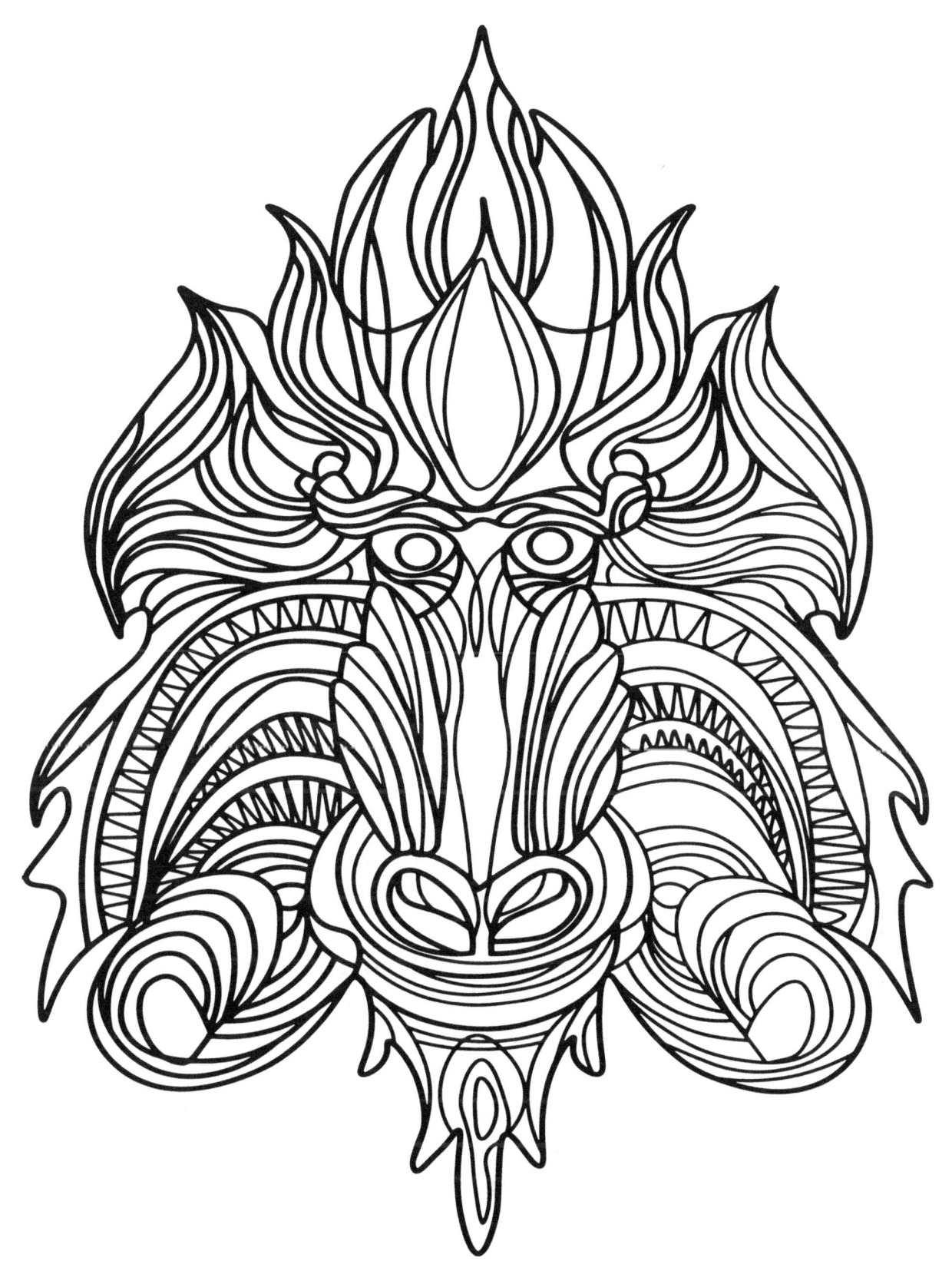

The leopard is native to 35 African countries, and is the most secretive and elusive of the big cats. With its striking coat and thick power neckline, it is easily recognisable and the strongest of the big cats. The lifespan of a leopard in the wild is around 12-17 years. Their habitat range is quite diverse, ranging between rainforests, grasslands, mountains, and desert terrains.

Leopards are predominately solitary animals with large territories. They mark their ranges with urine and leave claw marks on trees, as a warning for others to stay away. They are renowned climbers, and can climb trees even with the heaviest of prey.

Leopards tend to have 2-3 cubs per gestation cycle. Cubs suckle for around 3 months, and are kept hidden for the first 8 weeks, to protect them from predators. Throughout history, leopards have been depicted in artwork, mythology, and folklore in numerous countries. They are also now commonly used as an emblem of sports in much of Africa.

Because of their beautiful coats, leopards have been hunted for the longest time. Their soft fur has been used to make coats and ceremonial robes. People also hunt them for their claws, whiskers, and tails, which are popular as fetishes. They are near threatened on the AWF conservation list.

When brought into close contact with human settlements, leopards may prey on livestock. Pastoralists will retaliate and kill leopards in retribution, or will attempt to exterminate leopards, in a move to protect livestock killings.

These powerful creatures, with their majestic coats, need to be protected against poaching now, before they too may become critically threatened to the point of extinction. We must act now before its too late.

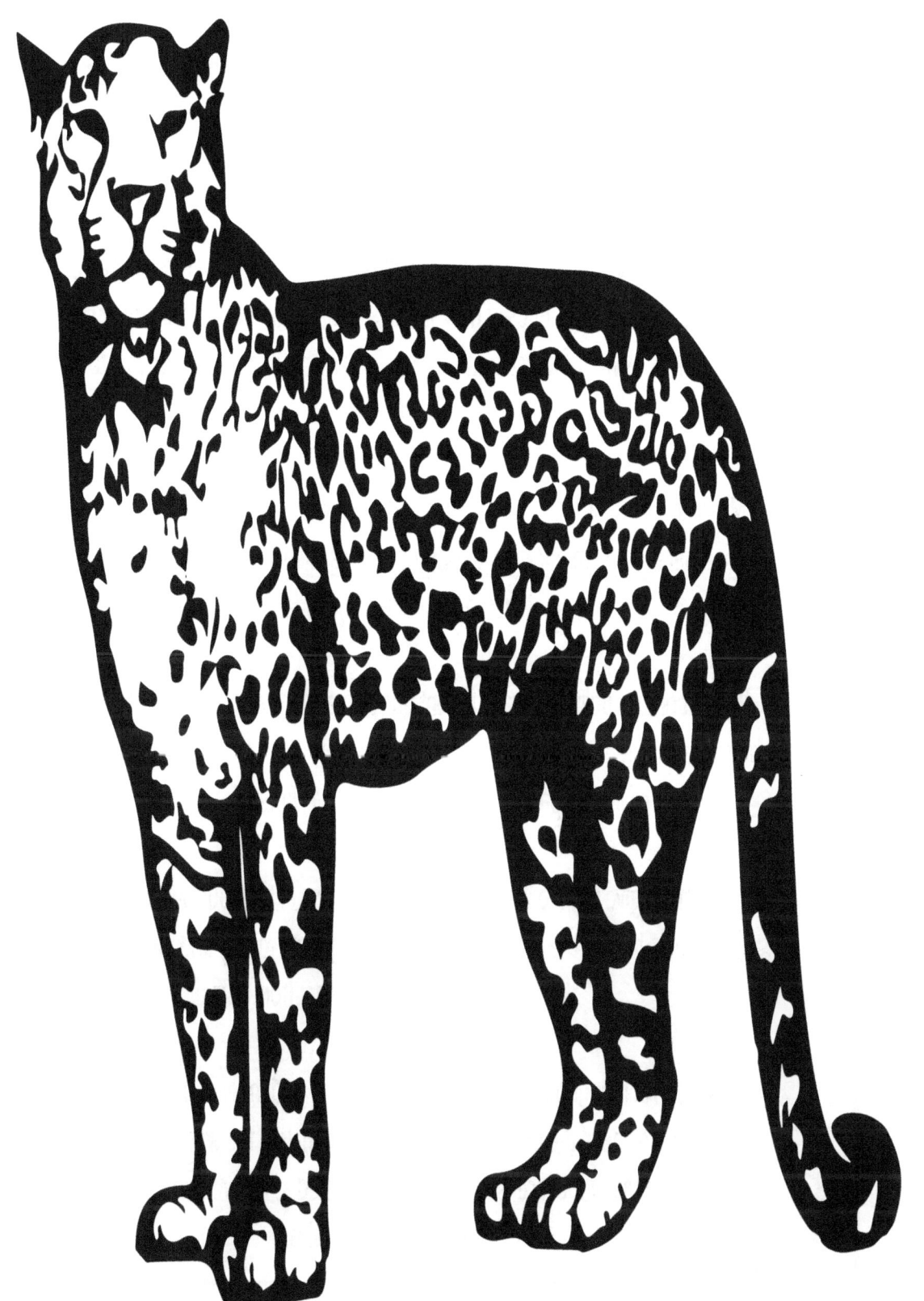

Meerkats are a highly sociable species, that live in large family groups. They may be small, but what they lack in size, they make up for in brains. Meerkats are mongooses, famed for their upright posture. They often stand on their rear legs and gaze alerty over the African plains, always on the lookout for predators. Birds of prey such as the hawk, or the eagle, are their main predators from the skies, as well as big cats and snakes. Each member has ther own role to play in the group.

Meerkats will eat insects, lizards, birds and fruit. When hunting small game, they work together and communicate with purring sounds. Meerkats are good hunters and are sometimes tamed to become rodent catchers.

Meerkat groups utilize several different burrows, and move from one to the other. Each burrow is an extensive tunnel and room system that remains cool, even under the African sun. They inhabit parts South Africa, Zimbabwe, Botswana and Mozambique.

Females give birth to 2-4 young each year in one of their burrows. Father's and siblings help to raise the meerkat young, teaching them to play and forage, and alerting them to the ever present danger from above.

No species of mongoose is said to be threatened or endangered thankfully. However, meerkats are one of the most strictly regulated animals in the world. They are illegal to own without the proper licenses or permits. It is listed as lower risk on the IUCN Red List of Threatened Species.

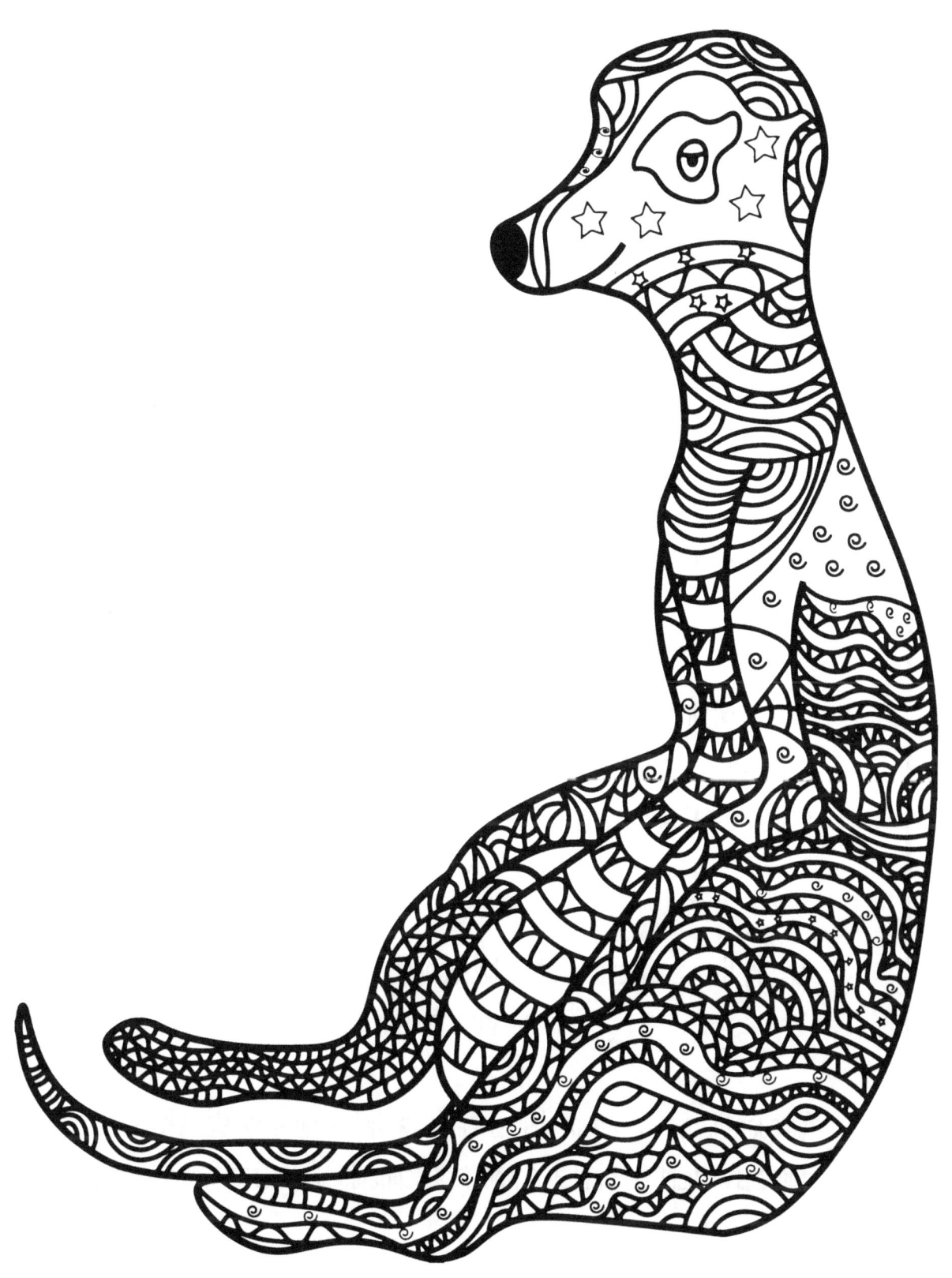

The hyena is one of the best scavengers in Africa. It is mostly known for its cackling scream, and its thick set appearence. The hyena is a carnivorous dog-like species, of which there are four sub species. The spotted hyena is the most common, with the striped hyena, the brown hyena, and the ardvark.

The hyena is a highly intelligent animal, and is one of the most abundant large carnivores on the African continent. Other predators view them as an irritant who would steal their hard earned kills. They are found on the savannah and the open plains, and live for about 20-25 years.

Hyenas group together in packs with the den being the centre of their territory. The hyena pack will tend to hunt for food as a group, and the hyena has exceptionally strong jaws in relation to the body size. Unique to hyenas, are their bone crushing teeth, and their main predators are lions, crocodiles and leopards.

Socially, the hyena lives in a matriarchal society. Females are larger and more aggresive and muscular than the males.

Although the hyenas are quite abundant in Africa, their conservation status is threatened. Humans will hunt and kill hyenas, whether its for trophy killing, or for livestock conflicts.

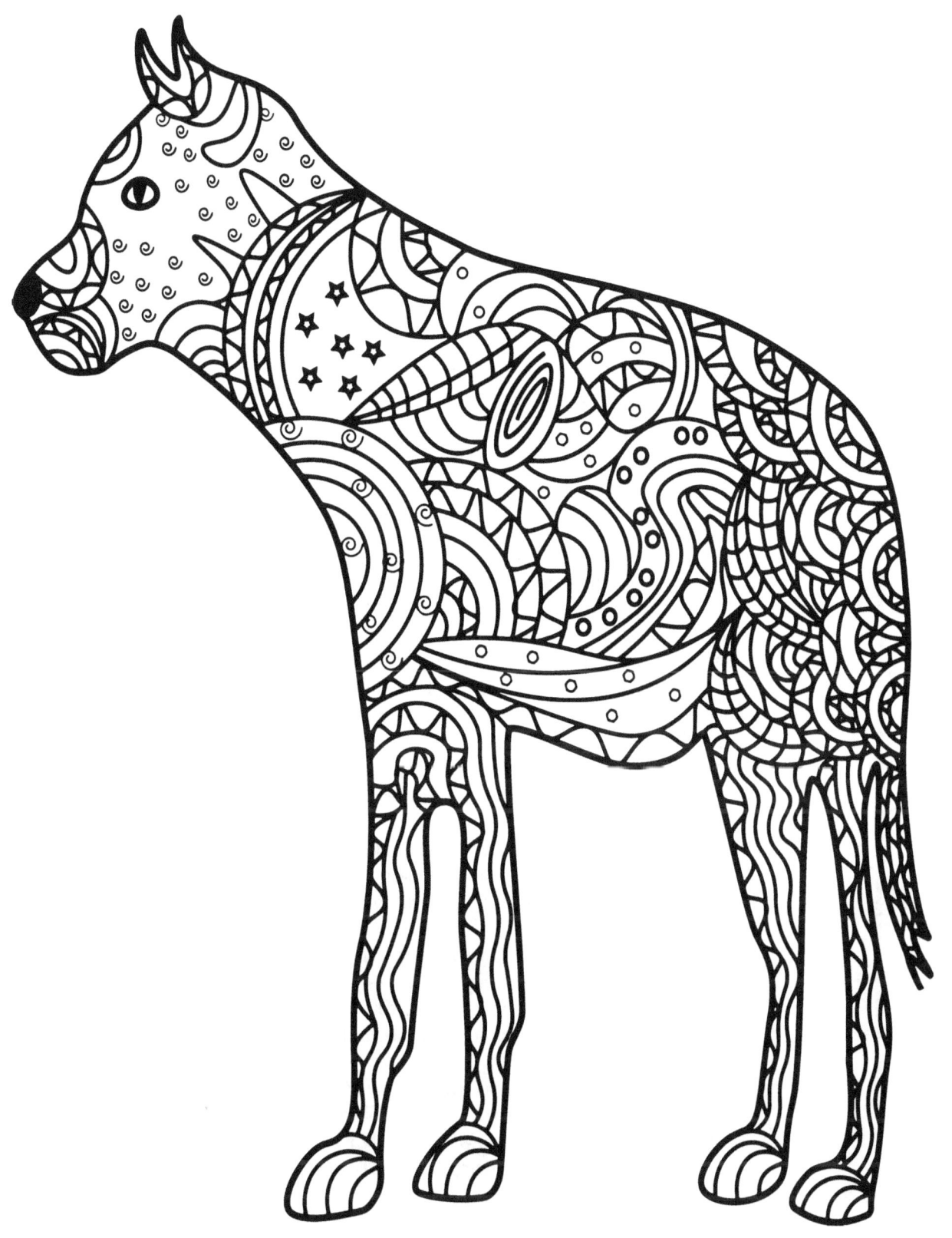

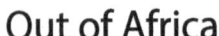

Out of Africa

From as far back as I can remember, all wildlife has completely fascinated me. I was always mesmerised by the magnificent country of Africa and all the animals that lived there. As a small girl, I loved to watch David Attenborough, and would dream of one day going to Africa.

After watching countless re-runs of Born Free, I fell in love with the big cats, especially the lion. I passionately believe that all wild animals should roam free, and not be held up in a zoo somewhere for us humans to stare at. In todays society, however, it is a sad fact, that zoos now play a crucial role in the preservation of many endangered species.

The poaching, and the mindless slaughter of innocent animals, horrifies me beyond belief, but it is happeneing every second of every day! One sub-species of Rhino is already extinct, while others are close to extinction. The magnificent elephants are also endangered thanks to poachers after their ivory. Each day brings new reports, and also some sickening images of the facts.

Belonging to the UK, and not extremely wealthy, I was tormented with how to help these animals. For the longest time, I have wanted to join the fight against poaching, but being a small minority and feeling insignificant, I did not know how I could help. Then, I suddenly realised, that if everyone had a mindset like this, then nothing would be done. But, if the minority rise up and actually try to do something, anything, then maybe we small people can make a difference.

So from this notion, I had the idea of putting together this book. Although it is not a huge book, it is just big enough for me to give you an insight into the facts. With a small selection of African animals, I want you to identify with each and every one.

Facts are facts, and the sad fact is that in my lifetime, maybe the elephant or the rhino will become extinct. Imagine not being able to show my grandkids the real thing, instead showing them pictures in a book. It is time to make a stand, and help in any way I can with the fight against poaching and the protection of such beautiful wild animals.

Proceeds from the sale of this book, will go to the AWF(African Wildlife Foundation), for the fight against poaching. It may seem to some like a small effort, but alas it is an effort. So please show your support for the AWF and join the fight against preserving our African wildlife. Lets stamp out poaching together.......

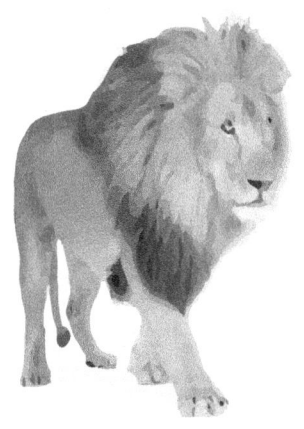

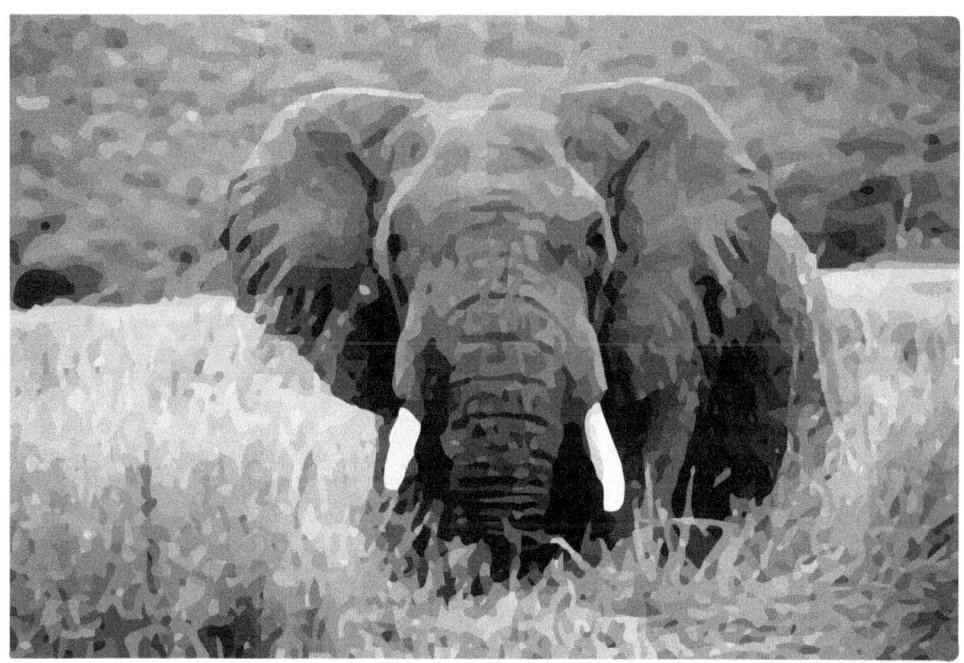

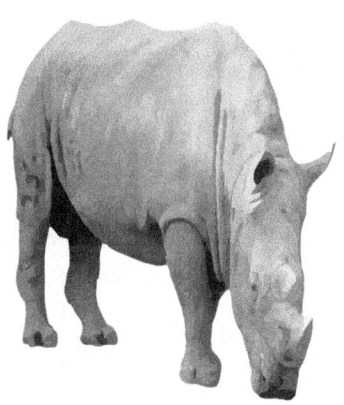

ISBN-13:978-1534895836
ISBN-10:1534895833